INWORDS

INWORDS

Journeying Inwards
with Ecclesiastes

Peace!
Sr. Mary Kraemer

Sr. Mary Kraemer, O.S.F.

Resurrection Press
Mineola • New York

Also by the author:

Abbey Press Prayer Notes
"Praying When God Seems Deaf"
"Facing the Darkness of Illness in the Light of Prayer"

First published in April, 1995 by

Resurrection Press, Ltd.
P.O. Box 248
Williston Park, NY 11596

ISBN 1-878718-26-6

Illustrations by Dorothy Noud.

Cover design by John Murello.

Printed in the United States of America.

Ecclesiastes
(Chapter 3:1–8)

*There is an appointed time for everything,
and a time for every affair under the heavens.*

*A time to be born, and a time to die;
a time to plant, and a time to uproot the plant.*

*A time to kill, and a time to heal;
a time to tear down, and a time to build.*

*A time to weep, and a time to laugh;
a time to mourn, and a time to dance.*

*A time to scatter stones, and a time to gather them;
a time to embrace, and a time to be far from embraces.*

*A time to seek, and a time to lose;
a time to keep, and a time to cast away.*

*A time to rend, and a time to sew;
a time to be silent, and a time to speak.*

*A time to love, and a time to hate;
a time of war, and a time of peace.*

—The New Revised Standard Version

Lovingly dedicated in memory of my parents,
Kate and Greg Kraemer.
They spiritually nourished my love for words.
And to my great religious community —
the Franciscan Sisters of Little Falls, Minnesota,
who have given me the freedom and support to pursue it.

A very special dedication to Sefra Kobrin Pitzele,
a beloved friend and author,
who encouraged me on dark days
and applauded me on bright ones.
In spite of great personal pain, she never doubted,
nor let me doubt, that *Inwords* would be born.

Contents

Acknowledgments

Special thanks to all who listened or read these pages and offered their positive suggestions. It would take another book to name them all! I am very grateful to Dorothy Noud for her artistic ministry throughout these pages and to Shelley Robasse-Bishop for her typing and proofing skills.

Thank you, Emilie Cerar, my editor at Resurrection Press, for believing in this novel idea.

Thanks, too, to my religious community for their "cheers" as the work progressed. Sister Thomasine Schmolke, believed, as far back as 1956, that someday a book would come from me. Thank you, Thomasine, for that faith. My wonderful supportive friends and family were there for me as always and without them, this dream would never have become a reality. Joanne and Jim Crosson — thanks for keeping me "up and running."

Thanks to Saints Francis and Clare whose contemplative spirit urges me on to search beyond the shell of words. Finally, I thank the Holy Spirit for giving me words that lead inward.

Foreword

In his *Introduction to the Devout Life,* St. Francis de Sales claims: "Physicians discover the health or sickness of a man [woman] by looking on his tongue, and our words are true indications of the qualities of our souls."[1]

This playful, serious, small volume deals with words, words like *potential, shower, because, heritage, butterfly.* This text goes one step further by dealing with words within each word. Sr. Mary Kraemer reveals something of her soul as she dances with language and then offers each dance to the Lord in prayer.

Words have great power. They can divide or unite, they can freeze or scorch, they can bring life or death. Words carry our thoughts to those who are miles away; words convey our feelings and dreams to future generations. Thus it is well to crawl inside words and extract their juicy nectar, their nourishment for the mind and soul. To care about words is to care about the soul.

There is a warning in the introduction of this book: "this search for words can be contagious." Disregard this warning since some contagions are happy and healthy. A love and respect for words can only enrich the journey of life and faith. Would that this text were longer so that the spreading of this blessed illness might infect the larger world.

A Wisconsin scholar and poet, Ruth Mary Fox, has a prayer

---

1. St. Francis de Sales, *Introduction to the Devout Life*, translated and edited by John K. Ryan (N.Y.: Image Books, 1950), 132.

of her own that I sense has already been prayed in the heart of Sr. Mary Kraemer:

> Christ, let not one
> Unworthy word ever be born of me
> Who has understood a word's high dignity.[2]

The dignity of words arises out of their connectedness with truth. Words both express reality as well as become doors for a deeper insight to the mysteries of life. Words should be handled with care, as they are in this volume.

Some people write in that wonderful land between prose and poetry. At times language bends towards rational understanding and then, caught by a sudden gust of wind, swings towards the forest of poetry. *Inwords: Journeying Inwards with Ecclesiastes* is betwixt and between which adds so much to its appeal.

If you enjoy the sounds of words, you will delight in the following reflections.

BISHOP ROBERT F. MORNEAU

---

2. Ruth Mary Fox, *Some Did Return* (Fort Lauderdale, FL.: Wake-Brook House, 1976), 61.

Introduction

Welcome to this exciting journey! If you experience the joys and insights delving into words that I do, it will be a trip like none other you have taken.

Recently, a friend who knows my "love affair" with words, suggested I read; *Your Word is Fire — The Hasidic Masters on Contemplative Prayer* (Paulist Press, 1993). Passages like: "Each letter contains worlds and souls and the Presence of God. As the letters are joined to one another and form the words of prayer, all that is in them rises up to God," and "It is through the letters that the word of God may come to dwell with us," touched me deeply.

For years, finding words within words has been an integral part of my prayer life. As a spiritual director, I often suggest it to my directees. Their positive experience with this method as well as the urging of my friends is what brought *Inwords* into being.

Ecclesiastes, Chapter 3, verses 1–8, was selected as the vehicle for this adventure because of its all-encompassing message. The random words take shape when called forth by the varied seasons and soul searchings Ecclesiastes evokes.

As I ponder each word within a specific word, I look first at what it is saying. Then, a concluding prayer, using the words chosen, completes each reflection. These are written in the first person and I invite you to become that person. Pray into each word from the scenery of your unique life.

A gentle warning needs to be given: this search for words can be contagious. I sincerely hope it is for you! You will never meet another word in the same way.

> *"Think that the letters of prayer are the garments of God. What a joy to be making a garment for the greatest of kings. Enter into every letter with all your strength. God dwells within each letter; as you enter it, you become one with God."*
>
> —Your Word is Fire

May your pilgrimage *Inwords* lead you letter by letter, word by word, closer to *The Word*.

A Time to be Born

Ecclesiastes 3:2

Welcome

We ... This word of greeting and affirmation
starts by inviting *me* to unify diverse parts of myself
with the people around *me*.
My world extends from *me* to *we*.

Me ... If my *me* is feeling scattered or fragmented,
it is difficult to truly *welcome*
anyone else into my life.

Co ... This two letter word *co*
is the link that connects the *me* with the *we*,
opening myself to the larger world.

Come ... Again, an invitation,
a call to free myself from wherever, whomever or
whatever might be holding *me* back and move on.
It is God gently calling, "*Come*, my friend."

❀　　*Welcome*　　❀

God of *welcome*, teach *me* your limitless acceptance
of all who somehow touch into the *we* parts of my life.
You and I both know that
the most difficult person for *me* to accept is myself.
Give *me* patience to *welcome* all the facets of my being
"*co*" with you and to *come* to a better understanding
of my light side, as well as the *me* in shadow.
Only then will I be able to *welcome* the people, places,
prayers and pray-ers that weave the fabric of my life.
A *welcom*ing heart is a heart reborn.

Potential

Pot . . . This is such a mundane kind of word
just a plain old container of some sort — nothing fancy.
Yet without it, there would be a real mess!

Tent . . . Now we have a reel of pictures
everything from imagined *tent*s of Jewish people
wandering in the desert to modern-day ones
that are so perfect for everything from in-depth retreats
with my God to lazy days in the sun with friends.
But whatever the style, a *tent* is a protective structure.

Potent . . . This just brims over with hope.
Unlike *pot* and *tent* it has no real boundaries
unless I choose to build them.

Ten . . . Another term that sets limits
but is also used to describe perfection
as in "She is a 10!"

❁ *Potential* ❁

What an absolutely fathomless word this one is, my God!
You have gifted me with *potential*
that overflows all the *pots* and *tents* of this world.
My challenge is to never let any other person or thing,
become ends in themselves. The *ten* in this word is also
a reminder of the *ten* commandments — never obsolete.
With your grace, I can live up to my full *potential*
day by day.

Inspire

In . . . *In* this one syllable, two seemingly opposites
— *spire* and *ire* — join to form a power-filled entity.

Spire . . . "Something tapering to a point — as a steeple"
is the dictionary definition of *spire*.
My mind pictures the image of praying hands
joined, steeple like, in praise.

Ire . . . Three innocent letters form this angry statement — *ire*.
So much damage can be done by *ire*
if I let it rule my life.

❧   *Inspire*   ❧

Inspire me, my God,
to allow this cleansing word
to slowly permeate my being.
Let the *ire* I feel
toward past hurts *in* my life, peel away.
Finally free, my body and spirit can be
reborn and become a living *spire*
of loving praise pointed directly toward you.

Afraid

Raid... I need to *raid*
my emotional, physical and spiritual storehouses
and rid them of the fear that is so plentiful.

I... Only then can *I* give spiritual birth

Aid... and *aid* the multitude hungry
for my loving compassion.

Id... This is the part of me
that gives me psychic energy.
What does being *afraid* do to my *id?*

❀   *Afraid*   ❀

Thank you, fearless God, for helping me to see
how limiting and self-defeating being *afraid* really is.
Once I do this, I disarm it of its negative power.
Raid the sources of fear within me, including my *id.*
Aid the birthing of positive, decisive values.
Only then can my lopsided fear
become a multi-angled blessing.

There

The . . . *The* is one of the most frequently used words
in our English vocabulary!
In this example it provides *the* framework for other words.

He . . . Another often-used word
— *he* representing men —

Her . . . and *her,* signifying the women of the world.

Here . . . Now the *he* and the *her* give birth
to a safety net, the *here* and now.

❀   *There*   ❀

Ever present God, you are *here* in this second.
You beckon *the he*'s and *the her*'s to be attentive
to you now, *here* in this place.
Stabilize my flighty mind so that I too
will be *there* to *the* moment as it unfolds
its wondrous mystery each new day.
Morning breaks into many pieces —
each one awaiting my signature of acceptance.
Be "ink" to me, my God.

Become

Be . . . What a word of invitation!
I am asked to *be* all that I can possibly *be*.
That means letting go of my fears
and past failings.

Co . . . The *co*-joining of you and *me*.

Me . . . Who is this *me* you are calling to *become?*

❋   *Become*   ❋

I do embrace the *co*-ness,
the togetherness of this dynamic word.
I will accept my *me* and permit myself to *be*
all that I can *be*.
Become my constant source of new life.
Thank you, creator God,
for lovingly birthing *me* to *come* to you.

A Time to Plant

Ecclesiastes 3:2

Now

No . . . This little word *no* is a troublesome one!
It looks easy, but I find myself
wanting to say *no*
to the demanding *now* moments in my life.
I want to say *no* when the phone rings
and someone needs a listener. I want to say *no*
when my arthritic hands want me to stop writing *now*.
I want to say *no* to that inner voice
that's begging for prayer time.
There are also those frequent times when I need to say *no*
in order to establish healthy boundaries.

Ow . . . It also hurts to say "yes" to the *ow* moments
that daily challenge me.
Ow is an exclamation that I feel like making
when a *now* demand conflicts with my precious schedule.

❀ *Now* ❀

What a short, loaded word this is my *now* God!
Will I say *no* to the present moment, even the *now* second?
It is so easy to say *no* if I emphasize the *ow* part,
because you know how I hate pain.
Now catapults me across the barrier of indecision and fear.
Inspire me to look at this word backwards too — *won* !
If I can say yes, can truly live the *now*,
I will have *won* a battle — a challenge — of daily living.
Divine Planter, together let us sow the seeds
of *now* living, of *now* loving.

Share

Are . . . This is such a neat word, all generous God!
It is another call to action.
But before I or others can interact, each of us has to be
who we *are* — our unique, individual selves.

Ha . . . Next comes the ability to *ha,*
to laugh at myself and the things that happen to me.
If I can *ha* at myself in the positive sense,
and not take myself too seriously,
so many fears melt away.

Hare . . . That requires the willingness for me to become
the comical *hare* in that famed fable,
not in a demeaning way but by gently looking at who
I really am — all the parts of my complex self.

❀   *Share*   ❀

Thank you for this *shared* experience,
God of infinite *shar*ing.
It began within the safe comfort of who I am,
who we *are,* our own giftedness.
Flowing from that came the ability to *ha*
at myself and others,
especially at times when the *hare* is permitted
to take center stage. *Share* also calls me to accountability
where material and spiritual things are concerned.
Triune God, who *shares* your Divine Essence,
spur me on to generosity
as you *share* your trinitarian life with me. Alleluia!

Participate

Par . . . Often I am called to *participate*
when I'm not feeling up to *par*
and desire only to withdraw into solitude.

Part . . . One *part* of me wants to mingle, while the rest
yearns for a quiet place of reflection.

Art . . . It becomes an *art* to *participate* fully
in an event, exercise or discussion

At . . . in spite of my inner turmoil *at* that moment.

Pat . . . A more liberated me can then *pat* myself
on the back for courage and confidence.

Ate . . . Before I knew it, I *ate* up the negative excuses
for why I should not be involved.

❀　　*Participate*　　❀

Source of Life, you not only *participate* in my existence,
you cause it. But, your gift of free will makes me
responsible to be up to *par* on my spiritual sojourn.
At the same time, I rely on your constant guidance.
Long ago, I *ate* up all my reasons for lack of time with you.
You are the most important *part* of my life.
Sometimes I almost feel your *pat* on my back
as I pursue a difficult goal. This is an *art* I practice,
in my fumbling way, with every breath I take.
You are my *part*ner. You are my goal.

Before

Ore . . . There is a precious "metal" within me
—an *ore* called faith waiting to

Be . . . *be* brought to the surface of my existence

For . . . *for* "mining" and distribution.

Fore . . . But first, it must *be* in the *fore*front of my heart.

❁   *Before*   ❁

Genesis tells me that *before* creation you existed.
You planted within me, *for* me,
the precious *ore* of faith ready and waiting
to *be* mined, to come to the *fore* of my life.
Before my faith can be further activated and spread,
you and I must unite.
Grant me this grace, my infinite God.

Shower

How ... *How* do I manifest my total love for God?

Show ... The gospels and lives of the saints,
both dead and alive,
show me the way to plant these seeds.

Ow ... Weeds of *ow* moments
can easily choke out love's tender shoots —

We ... if I don't expand my *I* to *we* and become
more aware of my sisters' and brothers' needs.

Owe ... It is interesting to see
how one simple "e" can change an *ow* to *owe*.
How can I repay all my *owed* debts?

❀　　*Shower*　　❀

Shower me, my source of all good things,
with the resolve to become a pray-er and a doer,
even though these seem to cancel out each other.
Exchange my *ow* moments for times
when I realize how much I *owe* you.
Show me, and my journey companions,
how we must live to extend your manifestation.
Shower me with your pulsating love.

Related

Elated . . . I am *elated* to be
on this spiritual journey to my God,
rooted in unfolding mystery.

Late . . . My all-forgiving one promises
that it is never too *late* to begin
living a God-centered life.
There is time now to sow new seeds.

Ate . . . What *ate* up my time in the past
so that my prayer life was so limited
or even non-existent?

At . . . But that is over.
At this moment I am new!

❁　　　*Related*　　　❁

I am *elated* to be *related* to you, God of relationships.
At each second of every day may our union deepen.
My spirit *ate* the Eucharistic banquet
and continues to do so.
I appreciate all the opportunities to get a fresh start.
It's never too *late,*
thanks to your generosity and patient understanding.
Perseverance is the kernel I need planted deep within me.
Then fears will not keep me from beginning
again and again and again.

Wandering

Wan ... There are so many *wan* —
listless people in my small yet global environment.

Wand ... Often I wish for a magic *wand*
to change all that.

An ... Such a *wand* would be *an* easy way out.

And ... *And* that is not how real changes happen.

Ring ... Awareness is the first bell that needs to *ring*
in my mind as I try to expand my horizons.
But it is not enough to break the
ring of indifference stored in my subconscious self.

❀ *Wandering* ❀

My thoughts are *wandering* in all directions.
Ring them with your truth —
that I am responsible for the *wan* members of your family —
not only the ones in my neighborhood,
but throughout the world.
The only magic *wand* that will accomplish lasting change
in the lives of people far *and* near
is *an* awareness and a caring that breaks through
the *ring* I have allowed to form around myself.
Sow expansion seeds in me, Divine Planter,
so that I will grow new world vision.
That is the blessing I long for and request.

A Time to Weep,

A Time to Laugh

Ecclesiastes 3:4

Devastated

Vast . . . That is exactly how the problem
that is facing me seems right now — *vast*.

As . . . I feel *as* if it is engulfing
my whole world, gobbling it up.

State . . . I can name the problem easily.
It is the illness of my very dear friend.
To let go of it, to allow God to have it,
seems impossible at this moment,
yet I know that it is all I can do,
and what I must do.
The word *state* also means a geographical area,
and the intensity of my fear and concern right now
would fill up the *state* of Minnesota.

Ate . . . This crisis *ate* up my usual level of trust.

✛　　*Devastated*　　✛

God of consolation, be with me and remove
this blanket of alarm and sadness that envelops me
as it does my friend.
Help us both to clearly *state* our fears to you
with total confidence. It seems a long time
since I *ate* from your consoling banquet,
but it is you and you alone who can take
my most *devastated* self and restore me to hope.
This is my plea. This is my prayer.

Bear

Be . . . Another instance when I am clearly told
to *be* 100 percent me.

Ear . . . The word *ear* leaps out at me
and joined with *be* commands me to *be ear,*
first of all, to myself,
to hear the nuances of the Spirit everyday of my life.
It directs me to *be ear* to all I contact,
to help people hear God's voice through me,
to cry with them, to laugh with them.
It also directs me to *be ear* to others
by listening — even beyond the words that are spoken.

✛   *Bear*   ✛

My ever-*bear*ing God, you challenge me with this word.
Bear with me, when I tire of being *ear* to others.
There are times, too, when the *ear* of my heart
becomes perplexed by the words of your Spirit.
Enlighten and strengthen me in those trying times
so I can *bear* with my sisters and brothers
during their sorrows.
You will always *be ear* to me.
Teach me your listening skills
that go beyond personal fatigue and pain.
Unstop my *ear*s from any blockage of prejudice
so that your *ear*s will *be* my own.

Shame

Sham . . . Sometimes my *shame* comes from
feeling like a *sham* — not authentic.

Ham . . . Lightness comes into this burdensome word.
There's a *ham,* an actor or actress that reacts, in *me* !

Ha . . . Empower me to *ha,*

Me . . . to laugh at myself,
when I feel the tentacles of *shame* grabbing *me.*

Am . . . I wrote this meditation several times,
and this teeny, weighty word, *am,*
stayed hidden to *me.*
That is what *shame* does,
it covers up, hides who I really *am.*

✛   Shame   ✛

This is a word that has plagued *me* all my life.
Now, the word itself presents the solution to the problem.
God of laughter and tears, release *me*
from the guilt and *shame* that can poison my life —
if I allow it.
You freed Peter and Mary Magdalen from their *shame*
and their sense of being a *sham.*
Let who I really *am* shine forth.
With my new ability to *ha* at *me,* to be a *ham,*
I will experience the same blessing of healing laughter.
Now I can love and serve you *shame*lessly.

Heritage

Her . . . What an inclusive language kind of word this is
starting with *her*.

He . . . I then remove one letter to get *he*.
We are all in this together, male and female.

It . . . What exactly is *it* that I am inheriting?

Tag . . . A playful word enters into this rather formal one.
Do I play *tag* with my *heritage*,
trying to avoid looking at *it*, claiming *it*?
Tag also means label.
Do I allow my *heritage* to put me in a box, limit me?

Age . . . Here's that word I hate seeing — *age*.
What is there about my present *age* that challenges me?

✢　*Heritage*　✢

The *he* in this word makes friends
with the masculine side of me.
Her embraces my femininity.
I belong wholly to you, my God.
It doesn't matter what my race or religion is.
The one *tag* that identifies me and all of us is — we are yours.
You are my *heritage* regardless of *age, age*less God.

Weary

We ... I come to this word with the combined *wear*iness
of my sisters and brothers — the *we* in my life.

Ear ... Sometimes, my *ear* is so full of concerns
that I do not hear God
calling me and all the *weary* to come.
"Come to me all you who labor and are burdened
and I will give you rest."

Wear ... And I *wear* my fatigue as a sort of badge,
forgetting that it often repels people from me.

✛   *Weary*   ✛

I come, *we* come, energetic God, to recharge
our *weary* spiritual batteries with your limitless energy.
Turn my *ear* from situations that *wear* me down.
Let your Living Word spark and revitalize me.
Sometimes I am so *weary,* I weep.
In my heart's *ear* I hear you accept those tears,
even applaud them.
I *wear* them as a sign of my growth.
With me comes all that my life touches.
We reach into your energy and are revitalized and renewed.

Joyous

Joy . . . This word dances before my eyes
and recalls memories of *joy*-filled times.

You . . . *You* and I, as people of God, are called to laugh,
sometimes in the face of seemingly
insurmountable obstacles.

Us . . . It is up to *us* to paint our God as a *joyous* God,
even when pain enters the picture.
But we are not asked to fake our *joy*.

✝   *Joyous*   ✝

An honest look at the *joy*ful mysteries in your life, Jesus,
shows shadows of pain surrounding *you*
even in the most *joyous* times.
How can we humans expect anything different
to happen to *us?*
Joyous God, gift me with an attitude of *joy*
that keeps bubbling up and spilling over
into every corner of my being.
Mary, Mother of *joy,* teach me how
to live even the sorrowful mysteries of my life
with a *joyous* spirit, rooted in your Son.

A Time to Embrace

Ecclesiastes 3:5

Message

Mess ... The first thing I see in this word is *mess!*
And that's exactly what some of the *message*s
I've been getting from God seem to be lately.
My life seems jumbled, chaotic, cluttered.

Sag ... Right in the middle of this word comes *sag,*
like it's so easy to do in the middle
of my job, my life, my prayer.

Sage ... Now this word, *sage,* I like!
Wisdom! It is what evolves if I only
search for it, recognize it, grasp it.

Age ... Are you telling me, my *age*less God,
that some of my chaos comes from *age*ing —
from moving on to different chapters in my life?
Is my life *mess*y because I am so resistant
to change — even to growth?

❂   *Message*   ❂

Yes, Divine *mess*enger, I do recognize the *mess* in my life.
I know it happens when I fail to live
into the wisdom my *age* can bring me.
Above all, Incarnate Wisdom, help me
to acknowledge you as *the sage* in my life.
May the *message* of this word lead me
beyond *sag* and *age*, to the "Yes" of Mary
when Gabriel came to her with a *message*
that changed the course of all our lives.

Drawing

Raw . . . Today, my insides feel *raw.*
My sense of purpose is weak and sporadic.

Aw . . . This is my sound of protest against my inner storm.

Draw . . . But then I hear my beloved speak within me.
"It is time now to *draw* on
all the resources within you, my child,
and *draw* on mine."

In . . . Calm begins to seep *in* as I feel God's arm
drawing my life together every second,
every minute of my life.

Wing . . . The nervous, doubting caterpillar in me
begins to form a *wing,* allowing it to emerge very slowly
from former chaos, fiber by fiber,
drawing ever closer to God, my source of wholeness.

Win . . . Now I am able to *win* this battle.

✪   *Drawing*   ✪

This began as a prayer of *raw* protest.
"*Aw,* why do I have to feel this way again?"
And slowly you led me to *draw* on your resources,
to look inside — to *win* this battle of sadness.
It ends as a prayer, reaching for the *wing*s
of power-filled love.

Because

Be . . . "To *be* or not to *be*" is a question
immortalized by William Shakespeare.
It is one I need to answer each day.

Use . . . Am I going to risk enough to *use* divine power
within me, to join forces with my God?

Us . . . Will I choose to remain isolated
physically, mentally, spiritually?
Or will I become *us* with my brothers and sisters?

Cause . . . What will *cause* me to stop
in the tracks of my daily life
and ponder these questions?

❂   *Because*   ❂

This is a covenant word, my source of all *be*ing,
even though it provokes many queries.
You promise to *be* my God.
I agree to join hands with the family of the world,
to become *us*.
Empower me to *use,* in the positive sense of that word,
what and who you offer me.
Then I will have *cause* to delight in you
because you will *be* my God and I will belong to you.

Reacher

Ache ... There is an *ache*, a hunger

Each ... in *each* of us as we travel
on our spiritual journey,
because we never truly sojourn alone.

Her ... I feel that *ache* more today,
as I see the agony of a mother in Haiti
looking at *her* starving child.

Reach ... I need to *reach* beyond
the narrow confines of my world
and embrace that woman and *her* child
with compassionate caring.

❂   *Reacher*   ❂

Stretch the *reach*ing span of my emotional
and spiritual love, *reacher* God.
It is so easy to become petty
and rooted in provincialism.
As I view that mother, help me to experience *her ache*,
so I am jarred loose from my self centeredness.
Each time I can *reach* beyond my 20-20 vision,
I, in reality am *reach*ing into your all-compassionate love.
I use a plastic *reacher* all day long
to extend my limited *reach*.
Be a spiritual *reacher* to me, my God,
stretching, expanding my global cloister.

Announcement

An ... As insignificant as *an* seems,
without it this word would not be itself.

Ounce ... My life is like that. Every *ounce* of me
has meaning and purpose.
The problem is, sometimes I fail to remember this.

Noun ... I stress the "verbness" — the doing part of *me*,
rather than the *noun* — the who I am.
I need to accept my unique being, embrace it, and

No ... say yes instead of *no* to my true self.

Me ... Then I am ready to *announce* my potential
within and around *me*.

Cement ... God's unconditional love of me
cements my "yes."

❂   *Announcement*   ❂

An angel came to Mary and *announce*d God's plan.
No would have been the simplest reply to that divine request.
But every *ounce* of Mary's being,
faithfully resounded a "Yes" that changed her life and mine.
Her body housed the *noun* of *nouns*, the Word become flesh!
You are the God of profound, earthshaking *announcement*s
as well as the minute-by-minute ones you make in *me*.
Shatter my complacency with the truth that you, alone,
are my God and I belong to you, unreservedly.
Cement this prayer into every atom of my being.

Palms

Pa ... An old time expression
but *Pa* still says it all
for many of us over fifty.

Pal ... Good thoughts of *Pa* would be of his being *pal*.
I'm blessed with memories like that.
I am keenly aware, though, of how *Pa*
is far from a *pal* to countless abused children.

Alms ... Having a *Pa* who is a *pal* is an *alms* — a gift.
This part of the word challenges me.
Alms does not necessarily mean money.
What *alms* am I giving to counter domestic violence?

❂   *Palms*   ❂

My God, you have carved me in the *palm* of your hands.
Thank you, who are my *Pa*, my dearest *pal*,
and my *alms*, for gifting me with this word.
I feel embraced by you now, even though
the carving causes pain.

A Time to Seek

Ecclesiastes 3:6

Search

Sear . . . What a multifaceted word *search* is.
It looks like a rather mild, gentle one
but then the *sear* part leaps out.
Sometimes, in order to really find meaning
in my daily happenings, I have to *sear* through
many layers of built-up excuses, fears, even resentment
before the real reason for my feelings surface.

Ear . . . And this requires keeping the *ear* of my heart
open and unplugged so that I will be able
to find the real answer
to whatever or whomever I am *search*ing for.

Arch . . . There is an *arch* in this word, too,
an entryway, a gateway to some difficult truth
I am *search*ing for.

✳   *Search*   ✳

It sometimes seems like my life is one
unending *search* party.
Help me to be able to *sear* through
the rubble of daily events
with my *ear* always attuned
to your subtle whisperings and graces.
I depend on you to guide me through my diverse *arch*es,
avoiding obstacles that would block
my *search* for union with you.

Believe

Be . . . *I* am called — no — commanded
to *be* at peace with my "*be*-ness,"

I . . . with who *I* am, before *I* can truly *believe*
in anyone or anything else.

Lie . . . Yes, there is a *lie* within this word, too.
It is a *lie* when *I* tell myself
that *I* am not good, beautiful, or lovable.
It is a *lie* when *I* do not accept my specialness.

Eve . . . This word calls me to evaluate,
every *eve*ning of my life.
Have *I* allowed self *lie*s to weaken
the fiber of my belief today?

✶   *Believe*   ✶

This word challenges me, my *believe*d One.
It demands that *I* tell the truth, not *lie* about who *I* am.
It dares me to *be* all that *I* can honestly *be,*
to *be* one hundred percent *Eve* — woman —
so that when the final *eve* of my life arrives,
what *I believe,* who *I believe* in,
will become the bridge that carries me
from this temporary life to our everlasting one.

Courage

Our ... Sometimes I feel like the cowardly lion.
Then this word jogs me to remember
that I am not alone on this earthly journey.
It is *our* adventure.
The Incarnation has transformed a singular yearning
into a duet of praise.

Rage ... But, when I see all the injustices rampant in
today's world, *rage* fills my soul.

Rag ... Then there are moments when I feel like
a listless and powerless *rag*.
But a *rag* can be a positive instrument too!

Age ... From the moment of conception until I die,
whatever my *age,*
I am called beyond my capabilities.
God's divine strength is readily available.

✳   *Courage*   ✳

Courageous God, you are beside me
on *our* journey, whether I am *rage*-filled
or *rag*-like, regardless of my *age.*
Give me the *courage* "to accept the things
I cannot change and to change the things I can."

Please

Plea . . . This is a strong beginning for a word
I use automatically, but the reality is — it is powerful.
I have to realize its strength.

Lease . . . I desire help to get a new *lease*
on both spiritual and physical relationships,

As . . . *as* my life unfolds.

Ease . . . My harried nature must *ease* up.
I need to take time to enjoy life's beauty and bounty.

✳   *Please*   ✳

This is my *plea,* my cry to you. *Please* my God,
gift me with insight into the truth of the meanings of *please,*
which also means "to be agreeable with."
Ease my anxieties and my tendency to be a people *please*r,
as I so often am.
Strengthen my new *lease* on life.
Root me in your pleasure, your peace,
so that the fruits of my being will *please* you forever.

Penetrate

Pen . . . With *pen* in hand, I feel totally free.
That's ironic because another definition of *pen*
is a jail-like cell.

Net . . . Why do I need and want constant reassurance
of my *net* worth? This need really does *pen* me in.

Rate . . . My heart *rate* speeds up as I consider the power
this word can have in my life, if I only permit it.

✳ *Penetrate* ✳

Penetrate the lightest and darkest parts of me, my God.
I thank you for the gift a *pen* is in my life and ask
for your *penetrat*ing grace to remove the *pen*s within me
that house things that can only harm me.
I also entrust you to *rate* me with mercy, not justice.
Net my talents, forgive my faults.

Imaginative

I ... *I* am called to my own Epiphany — my "God-insight."

Magi ... Beckoned by the *magi, I* allow myself to be led.

In ... The knowledge of this fact frightens me.
In my head, *I* am terrified.

At ... *In* my heart, *I* am *at* peace.

Native ... Only if I let go of my *native* surroundings
can I be guided by that star.

✳ *Imaginative* ✳

My *imaginative* God, the *magi* let go
of the fear *in* their beings
and *at* your decreed time were led *in* your chosen way.
It meant leaving their *native* security
and facing the terrifying unknown.
I ask to be blessed with that gift.

Researcher

Sea . . . I remember as a little child finding a *sea*shell and

Ear . . . holding it to my *ear*
expecting to hear the roar of the ocean.

Sear . . . How can I *sear* through the dross of memories
and return to the innocence of a child?

Arch . . . Childlike, I will re-enter the *arch* of adulthood.

Archer . . . And pray that the divine *archer*
will penetrate and unify all of me.

Research . . . It does not take a great deal of *research*
to uncover God's never-ending love for the total me.

Search . . . No matter how long I *search,*
my heart will be restless until it rests solely in my God.

❋   *Researcher*   ❋

This word calls me, *researcher* God,
back to my childhood when I held a *sea*shell to my *ear*
and expected an awesome result.
Sear through my adult layers of resistance,
mystical *archer,* to find my innate trusting love.
It doesn't require much *research* to discover
my unmet needs.
Fill the empty spots you *search* out
with your gentle influence and unlimited understanding.

A Time to Love

Ecclesiastes 3:8

Called

All ... My *all*-together God has gifted me with insight
into this love-song word.

Call ... It is definitely a *call* to each part of my being —
even the most fragmented ones —
to remember who is in charge,
no matter how I may feel at this present moment.

Led ... I have been *led* out of the various
"Egypts" of my life,
out of the bondage and slavery of selfishness.
Such is the power of my *call*.

♥   Called   ♥

What a motivating word this is!
First of all, it challenges *all* of me to be *led*
by your Spirit, out of whatever is keeping me a slave.
Maybe it is my lack of self-confidence
or my inability to always trust you.
Called is a word emanating from your unconditional
love of me, for me.
I truly believe you have *called* me, *led all* of me,
out of darkness into the Light who is yourself.

Forward

Or . . . Immediately, I am challenged.
Will I move *forward or* back?

For . . . *For* my God constantly calls me
to live a life of love.

War . . . That is a choice I alone can make.
If I choose to be at constant *war* within
and outside of myself,
I remove myself from nurturing, all-encompassing love.

Ward . . . *Ward* also means "one under
the care of a guardian."
I ultimately want to be a *ward*
of only my creator-lover, God.

♥   *Forward*   ♥

Steeped in your love I will be able to live
for you alone — there is no either/*or* about it.
It is also the way to meet head-on the *war* of good and evil
within me. Together, you and I can *ward* off
the negative influences around me.
Using the positive ones, my guardian God, I will be love
motivated *forward* into the encompassing *ward*
of your loving heart.

Heart

Hear ... My goal is to *hear* God speak in every
action and reaction of my life.

Ear ... This requires the *ear* of my *heart* to be unblocked,
physically and spiritually.

Art ... Now comes the *art* of *hear*ing,
to hone my listening skills so that I become an *art*ist,
sculpting what I *hear* into a monument of attention.

♥   *Heart*   ♥

Hear me, my listening God, and bless me
with the *art* of *hear*ing you and all my sisters and brothers
with the *ear* of my *heart*.
Delving into this word has made me more aware than ever
of the power of "love listening."
I promise to continue developing that *art* in my life
with your ever-present guidance.

Encountered

Count . . . I *count* in the eyes of my God!

Counter . . . No matter which negative thought
I *counter* that truth with, the result is the same.
I am very much loved and lovable.
I am special.

Red . . . A color like *red* may seem
to have nothing to do with the value of who I am.
But it can accentuate or underline
the veracity of the statement.

♥   *Encountered*   ♥

In this word I have *encountered* many indisputable truths.
Most of all, I again realize your unconditional love for me
that *count*s as the greatest gift I have received.
It is a *red*-letter reality.
Counter my self doubts with your constant,
all-encompassing presence.
Being steeped in this word leads me to *count* my blessings
as a redeemed child belonging to you alone.
What a heart-expanding thought,
encountered God.

Blessings

Bless . . . *Blessings* is a word I use frequently.
But what does it really mean to *bless* someone?

Less . . . Maybe it's necessary to start with the *less* part
of the word. Even when I feel *less* than others,
the reality is different.

Les . . . My brother-in-law was named *Les*.
He has been dead several years
but his memory still *bless*es us as a family.

Sin . . . *Sin* is a strange idea to find *in* a positive word
like *blessings,* but it reminds me that *blessings* can come
from even my shadowy, *sin*ful side if I permit it.

In . . . The challenge of this word is to find *blessings*
in every part of my life.

Sing . . . And then *sing* a song of gratitude.

♥   *Blessings*   ♥

Bless is such an easy thing to say.
It has taken me on an inner journey and made me realize
that it is permissible to sometimes feel *less* than positive.
On those days it challenges me to dig
in to the *blessings* within and around me,
not allowing my *sin*s to block the reality of your presence.
Thank you for the *blessings Les* still is to my family.
Now my soul *sings* joyfully, *blessing* others through you.

Accompany

Company . . . *Company* paints pictures of friendly visitors.
It also designates the name of *an* organization.

Pan . . . God is my view finder as I *pan* the vistas of my life
and the *company* I keep.

An . . . Then, *an* obstacle will become a doorway

Any . . . and my heart will be guided by
any impulse of God's spirit.

♥   *Accompany*   ♥

Accompany me, my God, as I journey through today.
Any person I meet can be *an* opportunity to *pan*
the gold of relationships.
How blessed am I to be in your *company*.
Continue to nurture me with the *company* of good friends,
who reflect your generosity, care and unconditional love.

Butterfly

Utter . . . The *butterfl*ies on the pages of this book
utter a final wish and loving prayer.

But . . . By their presence in varying stages,
they show that life is changed *but* not taken away,
even when it looks like death is imminent.

Fly . . . Their freedom to *fly* is earned by breaking through
a hard, seemingly unbreakable cocoon.
That too, is the challenge for each of us as we struggle
out of our personal "cocoons" to liberation.

♥   *Butterfly*   ♥

God of a single *butterfly* as well as trillions of them,
it is my prayer that each person who has read these pages
may find themselves *utter*ing a "yes"
of total acceptance of themselves, no matter which
verse of Ecclesiastes, their life experience finds them in.
But more than saying "yes" may they live into it
fueled by the power gleaned from *Inwords*.
Grace each reader with the freedom to *fly*
beyond any limitations
so that the journey inwards through *Inwords*
will lead them to become that "yes"
on their journeys with and to you, THE WORD. Amen.

Published by Resurrection Press

A Rachel Rosary *Larry Kupferman*	$3.95
Catholic Is Wonderful *Mitch Finley*	$4.95
Common Bushes *Kieran Kay*	$8.95
Discovering Your Light *Margaret O'Brien*	$6.95
The Gift of the Dove *Joan M. Jones, PCPA*	$3.95
Healing through the Mass *Robert DeGrandis, SSJ*	$7.95
His Healing Touch *Michael Buckley*	$7.95
Let's Talk *James P. Lisante*	$7.95
A Celebration of Life *Anthony Padovano*	$7.95
Miracle in the Marketplace *Henry Libersat*	$5.95
Give Them Shelter *Michael Moran*	$6.95
Heart Business *Dolores Torrell*	$6.95
A Path to Hope *John Dillon*	$5.95
The Healing of the Religious Life *Faricy/Blackborow*	$6.95
Transformed by Love *Margaret Magdalen, CSMV*	$5.95
RVC Liturgical Series: The Liturgy of the Hours	$3.95
The Lector's Ministry	$3.95
Behold the Man *Judy Marley, SFO*	$3.50
I Shall Be Raised Up	$2.25
From the Weaver's Loom *Donald Hanson*	$7.95
In the Power of the Spirit *Kevin Ranaghan*	$6.95
Young People and . . . You Know What *William O'Malley*	$3.50
Lights in the Darkness *Ave Clark, O.P.*	$8.95
Practicing the Prayer of Presence *van Kaam/Muto*	$7.95
5-Minute Miracles *Linda Schubert*	$3.95
Nothing but Love *Robert Lauder*	$3.95
Faith Means . . . If You Pray for Rain, Bring an Umbrella *Antoinette Bosco*	$3.50
Stress and the Search for Happiness *van Kaam/Muto*	$3.95
Harnessing Stress *van Kaam/Muto*	$3.95
Healthy and Holy under Stress *van Kaam/Muto*	$3.95
Still Riding the Wind *George Montague*	$7.95

Spirit-Life Audiocassette Collection

Celebrating the Vision of Vatican II *Michael Himes*	$6.95
Hail Virgin Mother *Robert Lauder*	$6.95
Praying on Your Feet *Robert Lauder*	$6.95
Annulment: Healing-Hope-New Life *Thomas Molloy*	$6.95
Life After Divorce *Tom Hartman*	$6.95
Path to Hope *John Dillon*	$6.95
Thank You Lord! *McGuire/DeAngelis*	$8.95
Spirit Songs *Jerry DeAngelis*	$9.95

Resurrection Press books and cassettes are available in your local religious bookstore. If you want to be on our mailing list for our up-to-date announcements, please write or phone:

Resurrection Press
P.O. Box 248, Williston Park, NY 11596
1-800-89 BOOKS